The
Wiersbe
BIBLE STUDY SERIES

The
Wiersbe
BIBLE STUDY SERIES

It's Always Too

Soon to Quit!

1 & 2 Timothy, Titus, Philemon

David C Cook®

transforming lives together

THE WIERSBE BIBLE STUDY SERIES: 1 & 2 TIMOTHY, TITUS, PHILEMON
Published by David C. Cook
4050 Lee Vance View
Colorado Springs, CO 80918 U.S.A.

David C. Cook Distribution Canada
55 Woodslee Avenue, Paris, Ontario, Canada N3L 3E5

David C. Cook U.K., Kingsway Communications
Eastbourne, East Sussex BN23 6NT, England

David C. Cook and the graphic circle C logo
are registered trademarks of Cook Communications Ministries.

All Scripture quotations in this study are taken from the *Holy Bible, New
International Version*®. *NIV*®. Copyright © 1973, 1978, 1984 by International
Bible Society. Used by permission of Zondervan. All rights reserved.

In *Be Faithful* excerpts, unless otherwise noted, all Scripture quotations are taken from
the King James Version of the Bible. (Public Domain.)

All excerpts taken from *Be Faithful,* second edition, published by
David C. Cook in 2009 © 1981 Warren W. Wiersbe, ISBN 978-1-4347-6734-9

ISBN 978-1-4347-6510-9
eISBN 978-0-7814-0375-7

© 2010 Warren W. Wiersbe

The Team: Steve Parolini, Karen Lee-Thorp, Amy Kiechlin,
Sarah Schultz, Jack Campbell, and Karen Athen
Series Cover Design: John Hamilton Design
Cover Design: Veer Inc.

Printed in the United States of America
First Edition 2010

1 2 3 4 5 6 7 8 9 10

101209

Contents

Introduction to 1 & 2 Timothy, Titus, Philemon

Too Soon to Quit!

Timothy was not too happy in his church in Ephesus, and Titus was in a difficult situation on the island of Crete. To both of them, Paul wrote, "Be faithful! It's always too soon to quit!"

Paul used the Greek word *pistos* ("faithful") at least seventeen times in these three letters. The theme runs through each chapter: Be faithful to the Word, be faithful to your task, be faithful to the people to whom you minister. God is faithful! But don't get the idea that the Pastoral Epistles are only for pastors and other "full-time Christian workers." These three letters are for every Christian, every church member.

I have added a chapter on Philemon because what Paul wrote to him fits right into the theme of this study. Philemon faced a difficult problem with his runaway slave, Onesimus, and Paul's counsel encouraged Philemon to be faithful to the Lord in solving that problem.

As you study these letters, I want to help you understand the ministry of the local church and also encourage you to stick with it! If you and I are faithful to the tasks God has given us, then His work will prosper and His name will be glorified. Could we ask for more?

A Note about Paul's Life

Paul was arrested in Jerusalem around AD 57 and was confined to prison in Caesarea for two years (see Acts 21:19—26:32). Paul's voyage to Rome to be tried before Caesar started sometime around September AD 59. After a shipwreck and a three-month wait on Malta, he arrived in Rome about February AD 60 (see Acts 27—28). There he had liberty to minister.

Paul was acquitted of the charges and released. During the two years that followed, he ministered in various places and wrote 1 Timothy and Titus.

About AD 65, he was arrested again but this time put into a dungeon. It was then that he wrote 2 Timothy, his last letter.

The other collected letters, including Ephesians, Philippians, Colossians, and Philemon, were written during his first Roman captivity.

—Warren W. Wiersbe

How to Use This Study

This study is designed for both individual and small-group use. We've divided it into eight lessons—each references one or more chapters in Warren W. Wiersbe's commentary *Be Faithful* (second edition, David C. Cook, 2009). While reading *Be Faithful* is not a prerequisite for going through this study, the additional insights and background Wiersbe offers can greatly enhance your study experience.

The **Getting Started** questions at the beginning of each lesson offer you an opportunity to record your first thoughts and reactions to the study text. This is an important step in the study process as those "first impressions" often include clues about what it is your heart is longing to discover.

The bulk of the study is found in the **Going Deeper** questions. These dive into the Bible text and, along with helpful excerpts from Wiersbe's commentary, help you examine not only the original context and meaning of the verses but also modern application.

Looking Inward narrows the focus down to your personal story. These intimate questions can be a bit uncomfortable at times, but don't shy away from honesty here. This is where you are asked to stand before the mirror of God's Word and look closely at what you see. It's the place to take a good look at yourself in light of the lesson and search for ways in which you can grow in faith.

Going Forward is the place where you can commit to paper those things you want or need to do in order to better live out the discoveries you made in the Looking Inward section. Don't skip or skim through this. Take the time to really consider what practical steps you might take to move closer to Christ. Then share your thoughts with a trusted friend who can act as an encourager and accountability partner.

Finally, there is a brief **Seeking Help** section to close the lesson. This is a reminder for you to invite God into your spiritual-growth process. If you choose to write out a prayer in this section, come back to it as you work through the lesson and continue to seek the Holy Spirit's guidance as you discover God's will for your life.

Tips for Small Groups

A small group is a dynamic thing. One week it might seem like a group of close-knit friends. The next it might seem more like a group of uncomfortable strangers. A small-group leader's role is to read these subtle changes and adjust the tone of the discussion accordingly.

Small groups need to be safe places for people to talk openly. It is through shared wrestling with difficult life issues that some of the greatest personal growth is discovered. But in order for the group to feel safe, participants need to know it's okay *not* to share sometimes. Always invite honest disclosure, but never force someone to speak if he or she isn't comfortable doing so. (A savvy leader will follow up later with a group member who isn't comfortable sharing in a group setting to see if a one-on-one discussion is more appropriate.)

Have volunteers take turns reading excerpts from Scripture or from the commentary. The more each person is involved even in the mundane tasks, the more they'll feel comfortable opening up in more meaningful ways.

The leader should watch the clock and keep the discussion moving. Sometimes there may be more Going Deeper questions than your group can cover in your available time. If you've had a fruitful discussion, it's okay to move on without finishing everything. And if you think the group is getting bogged down on a question or has taken off on a tangent, you can simply say, "Let's go on to question 5." Be sure to save at least ten to fifteen minutes for the Going Forward questions.

Finally, soak your group meetings in prayer—before you begin, during as needed, and always at the end of your time together.

An Important Job
(1 TIMOTHY 1—2)

Before you begin ...
- *Pray for the Holy Spirit to reveal truth and wisdom as you go through this lesson.*
- *Read 1 Timothy 1—2. This lesson references chapters 1 and 2 in* Be Faithful. *It will be helpful for you to have your Bible and a copy of the commentary available as you work through this lesson.*

Getting Started

From the Commentary

Timothy was born of mixed parentage: His mother was a Jewess, his father a Greek. He was so devoted to Christ that his local church leaders recommended him to Paul, and Paul added him to his "missionary staff" (Acts 16:1–5). Paul often reminded Timothy that he was chosen for this ministry (1 Tim. 1:18; 4:14). Timothy was faithful to the Lord (1 Cor. 4:17) and had a deep concern for God's people (Phil. 2:20–22).

But in spite of his calling, his close association with Paul, and his spiritual gifts, Timothy was easily discouraged.

Paul wrote the letter we call 1 Timothy to encourage Timothy, to explain how a local church should be managed, and to enforce his own authority as a servant of God.

—*Be Faithful,* pages 20–21

1. What clues does Paul give in the first two chapters of 1 Timothy about Timothy's tendency to be discouraged? (See especially 1 Tim. 1:18–19.) Why do you think Paul mentions that he has "handed over to Satan" Hymenaeus and Alexander?

2. Choose one verse or phrase from 1 Timothy 1—2 that stands out to you. This could be something you're intrigued by, something that makes you uncomfortable, something that puzzles you, something that resonates with you, or just something you want to examine further. Write that here.

Going Deeper

From the Commentary

One reason Christian workers must stay on the job is that false teachers are busy trying to capture Christians. There were teachers of false doctrines in Paul's day just as there are today, and we must take them seriously. These false teachers have no good news for lost sinners. They seek instead to lead Christians astray and capture them for their causes.

Paul used military language to help Timothy and his people see the seriousness of the problem (1 Tim. 1:3). *Charge* means "to give strict orders from a superior officer." Paul used this word (sometimes translated "commandment" and "command" in KJV) eight times in his two letters to Timothy (1 Tim. 1:3, 5, 18; 4:11; 5:7; 6:13, 17; 2 Tim. 4:1). He was conveying this idea: "Timothy, you are not only a pastor of the church in a difficult city. You are also a Christian soldier under orders from the King. Now pass these orders along to the soldiers in your church!"

—*Be Faithful*, pages 21–22

3. How does Paul's use of military language speak to an urgency in battling the false doctrines in the Ephesian church? What are some similar circumstances in today's church where a "command" to a church leader might be appropriate? What are the risks of not responding to the false doctrines swiftly and decisively?

More to Consider: Read Galatians 5:1–6. How does this passage speak to the "false doctrines" of religious legalism that Paul is warning against in 1 Timothy 1:3–11?

From the Commentary

The mention of "the gospel of the glory of the blessed God" (1 Tim. 1:11, literal translation) moved Paul to share his own personal testimony. He was "Exhibit A" to prove that the gospel of the grace of God really works. When you read Paul's testimony (see also Acts 9:1–22; 22:1–21; 26:9–18), you begin to grasp the wonder of God's grace and His saving power.

—Be Faithful, page 24

4. Review 1 Timothy 1:12–17. What do these verses tell us about Paul's testimony? What arguments does he put forth to illustrate the gospel of grace in his own story?

From the History Books

The city of Ephesus (in present-day Turkey) was at one time a city of nearly half a million people. Among other things, it was known for the Temple of Artemis (Diana). People came from far away to worship the goddess of fertility. The temple itself, which took more than a hundred years to complete, is often referred to today as one of the "Seven Wonders of the Ancient World" and is evidence of the strong pagan influence in the city of Ephesus during Paul's day.

5. What impact would the pagan environment have had on Timothy's ability to serve the church in Ephesus? What sorts of challenges might he have faced that were unique to a city that was known for its worship of a fertility goddess? How might knowing this about Ephesus have influenced the manner in which Paul addressed Timothy?

From the Commentary

It was not easy to serve God in pagan Ephesus, but Timothy was a man under orders, and he had to obey. The soldier's task is to "please him who hath chosen him to be a soldier" (2 Tim. 2:4), and not to please himself. Furthermore, Timothy was there by divine appointment:

God had chosen him and sent him. It was this fact that could give him assurance in difficult days.

—Be Faithful, page 27

6. How does Paul's personal story (1 Tim. 1:12–13) speak to the idea of being divinely appointed for the leadership task? How might this have offered encouragement to Timothy? How does this resonate with the way we view church leaders today?

From the Commentary

Timothy must have been greatly helped and encouraged when he read this first section of Paul's letter. God had called Timothy, equipped him, and put him into his place of ministry. Timothy's job was not to run all over Ephesus, being involved in a multitude of tasks. His job was to care for the church by winning the lost, teaching the saved, and defending the faith. Any task that did not relate to these ministries would have to be abandoned.

—Be Faithful, page 29

7. Why was it important for Timothy to focus on the local church? What greater value could this focus have had on other efforts to reach the Ephesians? In what ways do the leaders of churches today succeed in staying focused? In what ways does the church fail in this? How can Paul's words in chapter 1 help redirect a church that has lost focus?

From the Commentary

Often, what we think is the "freedom of the Spirit" are the carnal ideas of some Christian who is not walking in the Spirit. Eventually this "freedom" becomes anarchy, and the Spirit grieves as a church gradually moves away from the standards of God's Word.

To counteract this tendency, Paul exhorted both the men and the women in the church and reminded them of their spiritual responsibilities.

—*Be Faithful*, page 33

8. Review 1 Timothy 2:1–8. What were the spiritual responsibilities Paul described specifically for the men of the church? Why do you think he separated the responsibilities of men and women in this and the next

section? How much of what Paul described is specific to the culture of the time, and what can we derive from this passage that is universally helpful for all believers, men or women?

More to Consider: Read Matthew 6:5; Luke 18:9–14; James 4:1–10; and 1 John 5:14–15 to see examples of problematic attitudes some people bring to prayer. How does Paul's exhortation in 1 Timothy 2:1–4 speak to the concerns raised by these passages?

From the Commentary

The word translated "subjection" in 1 Timothy 2:11 is translated "submitting" and "submit" in Ephesians 5:21–22 and Colossians 3:18. It literally means "to rank under." Anyone who has served in the armed forces knows that "rank" has to do with order and authority, not with value or ability.

Submission is not subjugation. Submission is recognizing God's order in the home and the church and joyfully obeying it. When a Christian wife joyfully submits to the

Lord and to her own husband, it should bring out the best in her.

—*Be Faithful*, page 40

9. Review 1 Timothy 2:9–15. What are the specific responsibilities Paul outlines for women in these verses? What makes this passage somewhat controversial in today's church? Again, how much of what Paul writes is specific to the culture of the time, and how much is directly applicable today?

From the Commentary

Paul gave several arguments to back up this admonition that the Christian men in the church should be the spiritual leaders. The first is an argument from *creation*: Adam was formed first, and then Eve (1 Tim. 2:12–13).

The second argument has to do with man's fall into sin. Satan deceived the woman into sinning (Gen. 3:1ff.; 2 Cor. 11:3); the man sinned with his eyes wide open. Because Adam rejected the God-given order, he listened to his wife, disobeyed God, and brought sin and death into the world. The submission of wives to their own husbands is a part of the original creation.

—*Be Faithful*, page 43

10. What is your initial reaction to Paul's arguments about why men should be the spiritual leaders in the church? Why do you think Paul makes this distinction in his letter to Timothy? What can we discern from this that is applicable to today's church leaders?

Looking Inward

Take a moment to reflect on all that you've explored thus far in this study of 1 Timothy 1—2. Review your notes and answers and think about how each of these things matters in your life today.

Tips for Small Groups: To get the most out of this section, form pairs or trios and have group members take turns answering these questions. Be honest and as open as you can in this discussion, but most of all, be encouraging and supportive of others. Be sensitive to those who are going through particularly difficult times and don't press people to speak if they're uncomfortable doing so.

11. When have you been discouraged like Timothy? How did you respond to that discouragement? How can Paul's words of encouragement to Timothy help you?

12. Timothy was battling the false doctrine of legalism. How have you battled that in your church? In your own life? Why is it so easy to fall into legalism? How do Paul's words to Timothy help you understand the gospel of grace?

13. What is your response to Paul's exhortations to men and women at the end of 1 Timothy 2? How are Paul's words applicable to your life? Do you agree with everything he says? Why or why not?

Going Forward

14. Think of one or two things you have learned that you'd like to work on in the coming week. Remember that this is all about quality, not quantity. It's better to work on one specific area of life and do it well than to work on many and do poorly (or to be so overwhelmed that you simply don't try).

Do you need encouragement? Do you need to fight the temptation to be legalistic? Be specific. Go back through 1 Timothy 1—2 and put a star next to the phrase or verse that is most encouraging to you. Consider memorizing this verse.

Real-Life Application Ideas: Invite a discussion with other church members about how you can support and encourage the church leadership. Brainstorm specific ways you can encourage the leaders, and then take action on these ideas.

Seeking Help

15. Write a prayer below (or simply pray one in silence), inviting God to work on your mind and heart in those areas you've previously noted. Be honest about your desires and fears.

Notes for Small Groups:
- *Look for ways to put into practice the things you wrote in the Going Forward section. Talk with other group members about your ideas and commit to being accountable to one another.*
- *During the coming week, ask the Holy Spirit to continue to reveal truth to you from what you've read and studied.*
- *Before you start the next lesson, read 1 Timothy 3. For more in-depth lesson preparation, read chapter 3, "Follow the Leaders," in* Be Faithful.

Leadership Lessons
(1 TIMOTHY 3)

Before you begin …
- *Pray for the Holy Spirit to reveal truth and wisdom as you go through this lesson.*
- *Read 1 Timothy 3. This lesson references chapter 3 in* Be Faithful. *It will be helpful for you to have your Bible and a copy of the commentary available as you work through this lesson.*

Getting Started

From the Commentary

When you compare the qualifications given [in 1 Timothy] for bishops with those given for elders in Titus 1:5–9, you quickly see that the same office is in view. Church organization was quite simple in apostolic days: There were pastors (elders, bishops) and deacons (Phil. 1:1). It seems that there was a plurality of elders overseeing the work of each church, some involved in "ruling" (organization and government), others in teaching (1 Tim. 5:17).

But these men had to be qualified. It was good for a growing believer to aspire to the office of bishop, but the best way to achieve it was to develop Christian character.... To become an elder/bishop was a serious decision, one not treated lightly in the early church.

—Be Faithful, page 48

1. What sort of tone does Paul have as he discusses the role of the pastor (translated as "overseer" or "bishop") in 1 Timothy 3? Why do you think he opens his discourse with "Here is a trustworthy saying"? What is your initial reaction to the list of requirements/expectations for church leaders?

2. Choose one verse or phrase from 1 Timothy 3 that stands out to you. This could be something you're intrigued by, something that makes you uncomfortable, something that puzzles you, something that resonates with you, or just something you want to examine further. Write that here.

Going Deeper

From the Commentary

> It's clear that man's ability to manage his own marriage
> and home indicate ability to oversee a local church (1 Tim.
> 3:4–5). A pastor who has been divorced opens himself
> and the church to criticism from outsiders, and it is not
> likely that people with marital difficulties would consult
> a man who could not keep his own marriage together.
>
> —*Be Faithful*, page 49

3. What can you assume about some of the problems Timothy was facing
in the Ephesian church, based on what Paul says in 1 Timothy 3:4–5?
Why do you think Paul focuses on the issue of marriage and family in this
passage? How is this still an issue in the church today? Is it a valid concern?
Why or why not?

*More to Consider: If a church is considering new leaders, is it
critical that they meet the whole list of requirements Paul raises in
1 Timothy 3? Why or why not? Which of the listed character traits*

are most important for a leader? What other traits (not listed here) are important for leaders to have?

From the Commentary

> Teaching the Word of God is one of an elder's main ministries. In fact, many scholars believe that "pastors and teachers" in Ephesians 4:11 refer to one person but two functions. A pastor is automatically a teacher (2 Tim. 2:2, 24). Phillips Brooks, famous American bishop of the 1800s, said, "Apt to teach—it is not something to which one comes by accident or by any sudden burst of fiery zeal." A pastor must be a careful student of the Word of God, and of all that assists him in knowing and teaching that Word. The pastor who is lazy in his study is a disgrace in the pulpit.
>
> —*Be Faithful*, page 49–50

4. In 1 Timothy 3:6, Paul says that leaders must not be recent converts. What reason does he give for this requirement? How does this apply to the role of "pastor"? The role of "teacher"? How might that have posed a challenge in the early church? How is it still a challenge today?

From the History Books

Some of the most well-known preachers in history had little experience or training between their conversion and the first sermon they preached from the pulpit. One of the most famous is Charles Spurgeon, a British man who converted to Christianity when he was only fifteen and preached his first sermon just a year later. At nineteen, he was called to be the pastor of the New Market Chapel in London. Spurgeon reportedly preached to millions throughout his lifetime and remains one of the most oft-quoted preachers today.

5. How might Paul have felt about Spurgeon's youthfulness and fast track to the pulpit? What does this tell us about the guidelines Paul outlined in 1 Timothy? What does Spurgeon's story tell us about the way God works in the lives of those He calls to lead?

From the Commentary

Paul will have more to say about money in 1 Timothy 6:3ff. It is possible to use the ministry as an easy way to make money, if a man has no conscience or integrity. (Not that pastors are paid that much at most churches!) Covetous pastors always have "deals" going on outside their churches, and these activities erode their character and hinder their ministry. Pastors should "not [work] for filthy lucre" (1 Peter 5:2).

—*Be Faithful*, pages 50–51

6. Paul's note about leaders not being lovers of money is only briefly mentioned in 1 Timothy 3, but it seems clear he was addressing a specific concern in the Ephesian church. In what ways is this caution particularly appropriate today? What determines if someone is a "lover of money"? How have you seen evidence of this in the church today?

From the Commentary

The English word *deacon* is a transliteration of the Greek word *diakonos*, which simply means "servant." It is likely that the origin of the deacons is recorded in Acts 6. The first deacons were appointed to be assistants to the apostles. In a local church today deacons relieve the pastors/elders of other tasks so that they may concentrate on the ministry of the Word, prayer, and spiritual oversight.

—*Be Faithful*, page 52

7. What are the qualifications of a deacon, as outlined in 1 Timothy 3:8–13? How do these match up with the role deacons have in churches today?

From the Commentary

> A deacon should take his responsibilities seriously and *use* the office, not *just fill* it.
>
> The Greek word translated "degree" means "rank (as in the army), a base, a step, or rung on a ladder." What an encouragement to a faithful deacon! God will "promote" him spiritually and give him more and more respect among the saints, which means greater opportunity for ministry. A faithful deacon has a good standing before God and men, and can be used of God to build the church.
>
> —*Be Faithful*, pages 52, 55

8. What does Paul's testing of deacons look like in today's church? What does it mean to "keep hold of the deep truths of the faith"? What are those deep truths? How do the deep truths of the faith spur us to action?

More to Consider: Paul states that those who serve well "gain an excellent standing and great assurance in their faith in Christ Jesus." How does serving bring assurance in faith? Why is that important?

From the Commentary

Elders, deacons, and church members need to be reminded of what a local church is. In 1 Timothy 3:14–16, Paul gave three pictures of the church.

The house of God (1 Tim. 3:15a). God's church is a family, so "household" might be a better translation.

The assembly (1 Tim. 3:15b). The word *church* is a translation of the Greek word *ekklesia*, ... which means "assembly." It referred to the political assemblies in the Greek cities (Acts 19:29, 32) where business was transacted by qualified citizens.

The pillar and ground of the truth (1 Tim. 3:15–16). This is an architectural image that would mean much to Timothy at Ephesus, for the great temple of Diana had 127 pillars. The word *ground* suggests a "bulwark" or a "stay."

—*Be Faithful*, pages 56–57

9. Which of the three pictures of the church described in 1 Timothy 3:14–16 best describes the churches you have known? What are some ways congregants can know their church is succeeding as a household? As an assembly? As a grounded and safe place of worship?

From the Commentary

> The main truth to which a church should bear witness is the person and work of Jesus Christ (1 Tim. 3:16—it is probable that this verse is quoted from an early Christian hymn). Jesus Christ was God *manifest in the flesh,* not only at His birth, but also during His entire earthly ministry (John 14:1–9). Though His own people as a nation rejected Him, Jesus Christ was *vindicated in the Spirit,* for the Spirit empowered Him to do miracles and even to raise Himself from the dead (Rom. 1:4).
>
> —*Be Faithful,* page 58

10. Why do you think Paul ends this section on leaders and deacons with the reminder of Jesus' life and mission? (Read John 14:1–9 and Rom. 1:4.) What happens to a church if the leadership strays from this critical central focus?

Looking Inward

Take a moment to reflect on all that you've explored thus far in this study of 1 Timothy 3. Review your notes and answers and think about how each of these things matters in your life today.

Tips for Small Groups: To get the most out of this section, form pairs or trios and have group members take turns answering these questions. Be honest and as open as you can in this discussion, but most of all, be encouraging and supportive of others. Be sensitive to those who are going through particularly difficult times and don't press people to speak if they're uncomfortable doing so.

11. Have you ever been in a position of leadership in your church? Or have you been interested in pursuing a leadership role? How well does your character line up with what Paul writes about in 1 Timothy 3? What areas are your strengths? What are your weaknesses?

12. Consider the leaders in your current church. How well do you think they're doing in living up to the expectations presented in 1 Timothy 3? How can you support the leaders in your church so they can be successful in their roles?

13. No leadership is perfect, because no person is perfect. What are some of the things you can improve upon as you play the role of leader (whether at church or home or in the workplace)? How can you support those who lead you?

Going Forward

14. Think of one or two things you have learned that you'd like to work on in the coming week. Remember that this is all about quality, not quantity. It's better to work on one specific area of life and do it well than to work on many and do poorly (or to be so overwhelmed that you simply don't try).

Do you need to develop some of the character traits Paul mentions? Be specific. Go back through 1 Timothy 3 and put a star next to the phrase or verse that is most encouraging to you. Consider memorizing this verse.

Real-Life Application Ideas: If you're not already familiar with the role of deacons in your church (or other similarly tasked leaders), take the time to learn more about them. Consider inviting one or more of the deacon-level church leaders to dinner for conversation and fellowship and encouragement.

Seeking Help

15. Write a prayer below (or simply pray one in silence), inviting God to work on your mind and heart in those areas you've previously noted. Be honest about your desires and fears.

Notes for Small Groups:
  - *Look for ways to put into practice the things you wrote in the Going Forward section. Talk with other group members about your ideas and commit to being accountable to one another.*
  - *During the coming week, ask the Holy Spirit to continue to reveal truth to you from what you've read and studied.*
  - *Before you start the next lesson, read 1 Timothy 4. For more in-depth lesson preparation, read chapter 4, "How to Be a Man of God" in* Be Faithful.

A Pastor's Job Description
(1 TIMOTHY 4)

Before you begin ...
- *Pray for the Holy Spirit to reveal truth and wisdom as you go through this lesson.*
- *Read 1 Timothy 4. This lesson references chapter 4 in* Be Faithful. *It will be helpful for you to have your Bible and a copy of the commentary available as you work through this lesson.*

Getting Started

From the Commentary

Paul had warned the Ephesian elders that false teachers would invade the church (Acts 20:28–31), and now they had arrived. The Holy Spirit had spoken in specific terms about these teachers, and the prophecy was starting to be fulfilled in Paul's time. Certainly it is fulfilled in our own time!

—*Be Faithful,* page 61

1. Review 1 Timothy 4:1–6. What description of false teachers does Paul give in these verses? In what ways does the description apply today, too?

More to Consider: The term apostasy *is often used to describe the false teaching Paul was speaking out against. Simply defined, apostasy means "a desertion or departure from previously held principles." Why do you think apostasy was so prevalent in the early church? How is it prevalent today? Why is its allure uniquely compelling when contrasted with the allure of other religions or complete disavowal of faith?*

2. Choose one verse or phrase from 1 Timothy 4 that stands out to you. This could be something you're intrigued by, something that makes you uncomfortable, something that puzzles you, something that resonates with you, or just something you want to examine further. Write that here.

Going Deeper

From the Commentary

> [First Timothy 4:1] is the only place where demons are mentioned in the Pastoral Epistles. Just as there is a "mystery of godliness" concerning Christ (1 Tim. 3:16), so there is a "mystery of iniquity" that surrounds Satan and his work (2 Thess. 2:7). Satan is an imitator (2 Cor. 11:13–15); he has his own ministers and doctrines, and seeks to deceive God's people and lead them astray (2 Cor. 11:3). The first test of any religious doctrine is what it says about Jesus Christ (1 John 4:1–6).
>
> —*Be Faithful*, pages 61–62

3. Why do you think Paul opens this section of his letter by mentioning "deceiving spirits" and demons? What clues does this give us about the challenges facing the Ephesian church? What might Paul write to churches today about this very topic?

From the Commentary

> False teachers preach one thing but practice another. They
> tell their disciples what to do, but they do not do it them-
> selves. Satan works "by means of the hypocrisy of liars"
> (1 Tim. 4:2, literal translation). One of the marks of a true
> servant of God is his honesty and integrity: He practices
> what he preaches. This does not mean he is sinlessly perfect,
> but that he sincerely seeks to obey the Word of God. He
> tries to maintain a good conscience (see 1 Tim. 1:5, 19; 3:9).
>
> —*Be Faithful*, page 62

4. What does "integrity" of faith look like? What role does being "brought up
in the truths of the faith" play in building the foundation for integrity (1 Tim.
4:6)? Paul also mentions the importance of training yourself to be godly. How
do believers (especially leaders in the church) go about this training?

From the History Books

If you search online for articles about "religious cults," you'll find loads
of information to sort through. Though scholars from various religious
backgrounds have differing opinions on what designates a religious group

a cult, most agree on the basics. One of the most famous cults, commonly referred to as "Jonestown" (though it was officially called People's Temple Agricultural Project), is best known for the spectacularly tragic ending that came when followers swallowed poison-tainted drinks in an apparent "evolutionary suicide." The leader of the group, Jim Jones, displayed one common cult characteristic—a charismatic, compelling leadership style. People trusted him and therefore would do anything he asked of them.

5. How are people like Jim Jones examples of the "hypocritical liars" Paul writes about in 1 Timothy 4:2? What are some clues that help us discern whether or not a leader is a hypocritical liar? Do you think cult leaders are always intentionally misleading their followers? Why or why not? What would be a biblical approach to take if you were concerned about the doctrine or behavior of a church leader?

From the Commentary

> The emphasis in a minister's life should be on "the Word of God and prayer" (1 Tim. 4:5). It is tragic when a church keeps its pastors so busy with menial tasks that they have hardly any time for God's Word and prayer (Acts 6:1–7). Paul reminded young Timothy of his great responsibility

to study, teach, and preach the Scriptures, and to spend time in prayer. As a "good minister" he must be "nourished up in the words of faith" (1 Tim. 4:6).

—*Be Faithful*, page 64

6. What are some of the responsibilities Paul says are the hallmarks of a "good minister" (1 Tim. 4:6)? How have you seen these exhibited by the pastors and leaders in your church experience? Which of these responsibilities is easiest to measure? Which are more difficult to discern? What is the church member's responsibility in helping ministers to develop these characteristics?

From the Commentary

A believer cannot rediscover new doctrines. Paul admonished Timothy to remain true to "the good doctrine which you have closely followed up to now" (1 Tim. 4:6b, literal translation). He warned him not to "give heed to fables and endless genealogies" (1 Tim. 1:4). While a pastor must know what the enemy is teaching, he must not be influenced by it. A chemist may handle and study poisons, but he does not permit them to get into his system.

—*Be Faithful*, page 65

7. What is an example of "the good doctrine" Paul is referring to in 1 Timothy 4? How are leaders and churches swayed by bad doctrine? What makes it difficult sometimes to differentiate between good and bad doctrine?

From the Commentary

> Spiritual exercise is not easy; we must "labor and suffer reproach" (1 Tim. 4:10a). "For this we labor and strive" (NIV). The word translated "strive" is an athletic word from which we get our English word *agonize*. It is the picture of an athlete straining and giving his best to win. A Christian who wants to excel must really work at it, by the grace of God and to the glory of God.
>
> But exercising ourselves in godly living is not only profitable for us; it is also profitable for others (1 Tim. 4:11–12). It enables us to be good examples, so that we encourage others.
>
> —*Be Faithful*, pages 66–67

8. Earlier, Paul mentions the importance of being a seasoned believer before pursuing leadership. In 1 Timothy 4:12, he urges Timothy not to be discouraged by his youth. How are these two teachings related? Why does Paul note the importance of letting everyone "see your progress"? What are some ways we can be good examples for others (1 Tim. 4:11–12)?

From the Commentary

No pastor can lead his people where he has not been himself. "Such as I have, give I thee" is a basic principle of life and ministry (Acts 3:6). The pastor (or church member) who is not growing is actually going backward, for it is impossible to stand still in the Christian life. In his living, teaching, preaching, and leading, the minister must give evidence of spiritual growth.

—*Be Faithful*, page 68

9. Circle the things in 1 Timothy 4:13–16 Paul says make spiritual progress possible. What are some practical things people can do in order to progress in their faith?

From the Commentary

> [The term] *meditate* (1 Tim. 4:15) carried the idea of "be
> in them, give yourself totally to them." Timothy's spiritual
> life and ministry were to be the absorbing, controlling
> things in his life, not merely sidelines that he occasionally
> practiced. There can be no real pioneer advance in one's
> ministry without total dedication to the task.
>
> *—Be Faithful*, page 70

10. How do Christians today practice the sort of "meditation" or "devotion"
Paul talks about in 1 Timothy 4:15 in regard to diligence? What are the
challenges in today's culture that make this sort of focus difficult? What
are some practical tips for being diligent in matters of faith?

Looking Inward

Take a moment to reflect on all that you've explored thus far in this study
of 1 Timothy 4. Review your notes and answers and think about how each
of these things matters in your life today.

Tips for Small Groups: To get the most out of this section, form pairs or trios and have group members take turns answering these questions. Be honest and as open as you can in this discussion, but most of all, be encouraging and supportive of others. Be sensitive to those who are going through particularly difficult times and don't press people to speak if they're uncomfortable doing so.

11. Have you ever been tempted to follow teachings that are false? If so, what about the teachings (or teacher) was so compelling? If you have friends who are following false teachers, what are some practical, loving things you can do to help them see the truth?

12. What are some things you're currently doing to "train yourself to be godly" (1 Tim. 4:7)? In what ways are these things helping to bring maturity to your faith? Are there some things you want to be doing (or should be doing) but aren't? What will it take to implement these new plans? Choose someone who can hold you accountable to growing your faith and then pursue those ideas.

13. If you are young, how has that played into your faith experience? If you are not so young, how have you related to younger believers? In what ways can the young and old in Christ work together to build each other up in faith? How are you doing that now? How will you do that in the future?

Going Forward

14. Think of one or two things you have learned that you'd like to work on in the coming week. Remember that this is all about quality, not quantity. It's better to work on one specific area of life and do it well than to work on many and do poorly (or to be so overwhelmed that you simply don't try).

Do you need to do something to train yourself in godliness? Be specific. Go back through 1 Timothy 4 and put a star next to the phrase or verse that is most encouraging to you. Consider memorizing this verse.

Real-Life Application Ideas: If you don't already have one, find a mentor who has more life and faith experience, and start meeting with that person regularly to soak up all you can about the challenges and joys of growing in Christian maturity. Also, consider being a mentor for someone else.

Seeking Help

15. Write a prayer below (or simply pray one in silence), inviting God to work on your mind and heart in those areas you've previously noted. Be honest about your desires and fears.

Notes for Small Groups:
- *Look for ways to put into practice the things you wrote in the Going Forward section. Talk with other group members about your ideas and commit to being accountable to one another.*
- *During the coming week, ask the Holy Spirit to continue to reveal truth to you from what you've read and studied.*
- *Before you start the next lesson, read 1 Timothy 5—6. For more in-depth lesson preparation, read chapters 5 and 6, "Order in the Church!" and "Orders from Headquarters," in* Be Faithful.

Order and Orders
(1 TIMOTHY 5—6)

Before you begin …
- *Pray for the Holy Spirit to reveal truth and wisdom as you go through this lesson.*
- *Read 1 Timothy 5—6. This lesson references chapters 5 and 6 in* Be Faithful. *It will be helpful for you to have your Bible and a copy of the commentary available as you work through this lesson.*

Getting Started

From the Commentary

Paul admonished Timothy to minister to the various kinds of people in the church, and not to show partiality (1 Tim. 5:21). Since Timothy was a younger man, he might be tempted to ignore the older members, so Paul urged him to love and serve all of the people, regardless of their ages. The church is a family: Treat the older

51

members like your mother and father, and the younger members like your brothers and sisters.

—*Be Faithful,* page 75

1. What is the primary focus of 1 Timothy 5? Much of Paul's teaching in 1 Timothy is about respecting the older members of a congregation. Why was this particularly important in the early church? Why is it important in today's church?

More to Consider: Paul distinguishes between the older widows and the younger widows in 1 Timothy 5. Why this distinction? What can we learn from these passages about the culture of the time? What can we learn that is applicable today?

2. Choose one verse or phrase from 1 Timothy 5—6 that stands out to you. This could be something you're intrigued by, something that makes you uncomfortable, something that puzzles you, something that resonates with you, or just something you want to examine further. Write that here.

Going Deeper

From the Commentary

> "Guide the house" (1 Tim. 5:14) literally means "rule the
> house." The wife should manage the affairs of the house-
> hold, and her husband should trust her to do so (Prov.
> 31:10–31). Of course, marriage is a partnership, but each
> partner has a special sphere of responsibility.
>
> —*Be Faithful*, page 80

3. How does Paul's line of reasoning in 1 Timothy 5:14 line up with today's
cultural expectations and gender roles? What does it mean to "manage
the home" today? How does mismanagement of a home "give the enemy"
opportunity for slander?

From the Commentary

> Apparently Timothy was having some problems with the
> elders of the church at Ephesus. He was a young man and
> still had much to learn. Ephesus was not an easy place
> to minister. Furthermore, Timothy had followed Paul as

an overseer of the church, and Paul would not be an easy man to follow! Paul's farewell address to the Ephesian elders (Acts 20) shows how hard he had worked and how faithful he had been, and how much the elders loved Paul (Acts 20:36–38). In spite of the fact that Paul had personally sent Timothy to Ephesus, the young man was having a hard time.

—*Be Faithful*, pages 81–82

4. Read Acts 20. How does this passage shed light on the situation Timothy was facing with the elders? What does this suggest about the importance of the elders to Paul? To Timothy? What does "double honor" look like (1 Tim. 5:17)?

More to Consider: How might some people misinterpret the message of 1 Timothy 5:23? How does the context of this verse help to explain its meaning?

From the Commentary

> It is sad when a church member must be disciplined, but it is even sadder when a spiritual leader fails and must be disciplined, for leaders, when they fall, have a way of affecting others.
>
> The purpose of discipline is restoration, not revenge. Our purpose must be to save the offender, not to drive him away. Our attitude must be one of love and tenderness (Gal. 6:1–3). In fact, the verb *restore* that Paul used in Galatians 6:1 means "to set a broken bone." Think of the patience and tenderness involved in that procedure!
>
> —*Be Faithful*, page 84

5. Respond to the following statement: "The purpose of discipline is restoration, not revenge." How do Paul's words in 1 Timothy 5:19–21 validate this statement? In your church experience, how has discipline been meted out to leadership? Why do you think Paul encourages Timothy to rebuke sinners publicly? What benefit does that provide the sinner? The church?

From Today's World

Though the popularity of TV evangelists has waned in recent years, it's still not a real surprise when the national news reports about a televangelist's alleged financial improprieties. But below the radar of the stories that get national news coverage, you'll find plenty of "smaller" offenses in local church ministries—everything from mismanagement of funds to pastors spending "work" time pursuing greater wealth (whether that's pursuing a book deal or selling real estate from the church office). In many cases, these pastors are not intentionally trying to steal from the church; they're just trying to make ends meet in a profession that typically doesn't pay well.

6. How does the love of money (1 Tim. 6:3–10) negatively affect church leadership? How is anyone to know when "enough is enough"? What is the pastor's responsibility when it comes to money? What is the church member's responsibility in helping the leadership avoid falling into the "love of money" trap?

From the Commentary

Paul gave three reasons why Christian slaves should show respect for their believing masters and not take advantage of them. The most obvious reason is *their masters are*

Christians ("faithful" = believing). How can one believer take advantage of another believer? Second, *their masters are beloved.* Love does not rebel or look for opportunities to escape responsibility. Finally, *both master and servant benefit from obedience* ("partakers of the benefit" can apply to both of them). There is a mutual blessing when Christians serve each other in the will of God.

—*Be Faithful*, pages 90–91

7. How does Paul's message to Christian slaves apply to Christians in the workplace (1 Tim. 6:1–2)? Rewrite these verses as if Paul were speaking to Christian workers today.

From the Commentary

A believer who understands the Word will have a burning heart, not a big head (Luke 24:32; and see Dan. 9:1–20). This "conceited attitude" causes a teacher to argue about minor matters concerning "words" (1 Tim. 6:3). Instead of feeding on the "wholesome words of … Christ," you might say he gets sick about questions. The word *doting* (1 Tim. 6:4) means "filled with a morbid desire, sick." The result of such unspiritual teaching is "envy, quarreling, malicious talk, evil suspicions, and constant friction" (1 Tim. 6:4b–5a NIV).

—Be Faithful, page 92

8. Why do some people have an "unhealthy interest in controversies and quarrels"? How was that evident in the early church? How is it manifest today? What is Paul's answer to such people? What does Paul mean by "godliness with contentment" (1 Tim. 6:6)?

More to Consider: Healthy discourse often includes disagreement, especially when it comes to church matters. How do you engage in healthy discourse without slipping into unnecessary arguments or controversy? (See Prov. 25:6–12; James 1:19–20.)

From the Commentary

"They that *will be* rich …" is the accurate translation [of
1 Timothy 6:9–10]. It describes a person who has to have
more and more material things in order to be happy and
feel successful. But riches are a trap; they lead to bondage,
not freedom. Instead of giving satisfaction, riches create
additional lusts (desires), and these must be satisfied.
Instead of providing help and health, an excess of material things hurts and wounds. The result Paul described
very vividly: "Harmful desires … plunge men into ruin
and destruction" (1 Tim. 6:9 NIV). It is the picture of a
man drowning!

—*Be Faithful,* page 94

9. Circle the warnings Paul gives in 1 Timothy 6 about the dangers of
loving money. Why are these warnings particularly significant to the
modern church? How is the love of money the "root" of evil? (See also
Matt. 19:16–30.)

From the Commentary

The rich farmer in our Lord's parable (Luke 12:13–21) thought that his wealth meant security, when really it was an evidence of insecurity. He was not really trusting God. Riches are uncertain, not only in their value (which changes constantly), but also in their durability. Thieves can steal wealth, investments can drop in value, and the ravages of time can ruin houses and cars. If God gives us wealth, we should trust Him, the Giver, and not in the gifts.

—*Be Faithful*, page 100

10. What commands does Paul give Timothy in 1 Timothy 6:11–12? How does Paul encourage Timothy to lead others in 1 Timothy 6:17–19? Why are these charges to Timothy appropriate for today's leaders? What is the best way for leaders to teach others these truths?

Looking Inward

Take a moment to reflect on all that you've explored thus far in this study of 1 Timothy 5—6. Review your notes and answers and think about how each of these things matters in your life today.

Tips for Small Groups: To get the most out of this section, form pairs or trios and have group members take turns answering these questions. Be honest and as open as you can in this discussion, but most of all, be encouraging and supportive of others. Be sensitive to those who are going through particularly difficult times and don't press people to speak if they're uncomfortable doing so.

11. As you consider the advice Paul gives in 1 Timothy 5 about widows, elders, and slaves, what can you glean from this that is specifically applicable to your life and your relationships? What are some practical ways you can live out these truths?

12. How well are you doing in respecting the authority and maturity of the elders (or similarly charged leaders) in your church? What are some ways you can learn from the elders? What are some ways you can support them in their roles?

13. Consider your current perspective on money. Are you content in your current circumstances? Why or why not? In what ways does money lead to "evil" in your life? What needs to change in your perspective to avoid loving money more than you love God?

Going Forward

14. Think of one or two things you have learned that you'd like to work on in the coming week. Remember that this is all about quality, not quantity. It's better to work on one specific area of life and do it well than to work on many and do poorly (or to be so overwhelmed that you simply don't try).

Do you need to examine your perspective on money or wealth? Do you need to learn how to support the elders in your church? Be specific. Go back through 1 Timothy 5—6 and put a star next to the phrase or verse that is most encouraging to you. Consider memorizing this verse.

Real-Life Application Ideas: Take a week to focus on what it means to know "godliness with contentment" (1 Tim. 6:6). Talk with your family or friends about this pursuit, and brainstorm practical ways to be content with less material wealth while seeking God's wisdom. After this week is up, consider applying the lessons to everyday life.

Seeking Help

15. Write a prayer below (or simply pray one in silence), inviting God to work on your mind and heart in those areas you've previously noted. Be honest about your desires and fears.

Notes for Small Groups:

- *Look for ways to put into practice the things you wrote in the Going Forward section. Talk with other group members about your ideas and commit to being accountable to one another.*

- *During the coming week, ask the Holy Spirit to continue to reveal truth to you from what you've read and studied.*

- *Before you start the next lesson, read all three chapters in the book of Titus. For more in-depth lesson preparation, read chapters 7 and 8, "Our Man in Crete" and "How to Have a Healthy Church," in* Be Faithful.

Church Health
(TITUS)

Before you begin …
- *Pray for the Holy Spirit to reveal truth and wisdom as you go through this lesson.*
- *Read Titus 1—3. This lesson references chapters 7 and 8 in* Be Faithful. *It will be helpful for you to have your Bible and a copy of the commentary available as you work through this lesson.*

Getting Started

From the Commentary

While Timothy was laboring in metropolitan Ephesus, Titus had his hands full on the island of Crete. Titus was a Greek believer (Gal. 2:3) who had served Paul well on special assignments to the church in Corinth (2 Cor. 7:13–14; 8:6, 16, 23; 12:18). Apparently Titus had been won to Christ through Paul's personal ministry (Titus 1:4) as Timothy had been (1 Tim. 1:2). "As for Titus,"

Paul wrote, "he is my partner and fellow worker among you" (2 Cor. 8:23 NIV).

But the people on the island of Crete were not the easiest to work with, and Titus became somewhat discouraged. Like Timothy, he was probably a young man. But unlike Timothy, he was not given to timidity and physical ailments. Paul had been with Titus on Crete and had left him there to correct the things that were wrong. Since Jews from Crete were present at Pentecost (Acts 2:11), it is possible they had carried the gospel to their native land.

—Be Faithful, page 107

1. What clues do you have in Paul's letter to Titus that things aren't going all that well in Crete? What are the challenges Titus seems to be facing?

More to Consider: Crete is in the Mediterranean Sea and is one of the peripheral Greek isles. What would be some of the unique challenges Titus had to face because this island was apart from the mainland (and even from the main Greek islands)? What are the benefits of being set apart from mainstream culture? What are the disadvantages?

2. Choose one verse or phrase from Titus 1—3 that stands out to you. This could be something you're intrigued by, something that makes you uncomfortable, something that puzzles you, something that resonates with you, or just something you want to examine further. Write that here.

Going Deeper

From the Commentary

> One reason Paul had left Titus on the island of Crete was that he might organize the local assemblies and "set in order" the things that were lacking. That phrase is a medical term; it was applied to the setting of a crooked limb. Titus was not the spiritual dictator of the island, but he was Paul's official apostolic representative with authority to work.
>
> Several of the qualifications listed [in Titus 1:5–9] have already been discussed in our study of 1 Timothy 3:2–3: "blameless, the husband of one wife ... not given to wine,

no striker [not violent], not given to filthy lucre ... a lover of hospitality ... sober." The fact that these standards applied to Christians on the island of Crete as well as to those in the city of Ephesus proves that God's measure for leaders does not fluctuate.

—*Be Faithful*, page 110

3. What additional qualifications does Paul give leaders in Titus 1:5–9? Why do you think Paul focused on these particular issues?

From the Commentary

It did not take long for false teachers to rise in the early church. Wherever God sows the truth, Satan quickly shows up to sow lies. Titus faced an enemy similar to that described in 1 Timothy—a mixture of Jewish legalism, man-made traditions, and mysticism.

They would not submit to God's Word or to the authority of God's servant, for they were *unruly*. "Rebellious" would be a good translation. Beware of teachers who will not put themselves under authority.

They were *vain talkers*. What they said impressed people, but it had no content or substance.

—*Be Faithful*, page 113

4. What does Paul mean by "the circumcision group" in Titus 1:10? What does this tell you about the false doctrine that was infecting the church in Crete? Why do you think Paul quotes one of the false prophets, saying "Cretans are always liars, evil brutes, lazy gluttons"? How might that statement have been received by Titus?

From the History Books

The word *heresy* refers to the rejection of a belief or series of beliefs held by an organized or established religious group. If you scan the history books, you'll quickly learn that heresies are usually determined by measuring them against what have become orthodox beliefs. Orthodoxy itself has grown over the years, but the basic tenets of Christian faith have remained the same. In Paul's time, the doctrines of the church were still being developed, so any charges of "heresy" might also have been perceived by some as merely an alternate view of the developing doctrine.

5. What gave Paul the authority to challenge the false teachers and their heretical teachings? By what criteria did Paul (and the other early church leaders) determine if a belief was false? How are the challenges he faced in his day different from those facing today's church leaders?

From the Commentary

> It never ceases to amaze me what some people get out of the Scriptures! I was once on a telephone talk program on a Chicago radio station, discussing Bible prophecy. A man phoned in and tried to take over the program by proclaiming his strange interpretations of Daniel's prophecies. He rejected the clear explanation given in the Bible and was very upset with me when I refused to agree with his fanciful ideas.
>
> Dr. David Cooper used to say, "When the plain sense of Scripture makes good sense, seek no other sense."
>
> —*Be Faithful*, pages 114–15

6. In what ways does the message of Titus 1:10–16 make "good sense"? What does Paul mean by "To the pure, all things are pure, but to those

who are corrupted and do not believe, nothing is pure"? Some people look to Titus 1:15 as biblical basis for continuing in sin. How do they twist this passage in order to come to that conclusion?

More to Consider: Paul is specifically referring to food in this verse (see Be Faithful, *pages 115–16, for insight). Why would the topic of food have been significant to the early Christians and, in particular, to Christians who were being influenced by false teachers in league with Jewish legalism?*

From the Commentary

How easy it would be for a younger man like Titus to misunderstand or even neglect the older members of his congregation.

"I want a church of young people!" a pastor once said to me, forgetting that one day he would be old himself. A church needs both the old and the young, and they should minister to one another. The grace of God enables us to bridge the generation gap in the church. One way to

do this is for all members, young and old, to live up to the
standards that God has set for our lives.

—*Be Faithful*, page 121

7. How does Paul address the issue of age in Titus 2:1–4? Circle the traits
Paul encourages for "older men," and underline the traits Paul encourages
for "older women." How are they similar? How are they different? What
do these lists tell us about the culture of the time? How are these truths
applicable today?

From the Commentary

The greatest priority in a home should be love. If a wife
loved her husband and her children, she was well on the
way to making the marriage and the home a success. In
our Western society, a man and a woman fall in love and
then get married, but in the East, marriages were less
romantic. Often the two got married and then had to
learn to love each other.

—*Be Faithful*, page 123

8. In Titus 2:4–8, Paul turns his focus to "younger women" and "young men." What specific advice does he give these groups? How does this differ from the wisdom he offers to older men and women? He encourages both the women and the men to be "self-controlled." What does self-control look like in practical terms?

More to Consider: In what ways does Titus 2:7b–8 describe integrity? How important was consistency of character in the growth of the early church? Why is it so important today, too?

From the Commentary

The Greek word *tupos* ("pattern," Titus 2:7) gives us our English word *type*. The word originally meant "an impression made by a die." Titus was to live so that his life would be like a "spiritual die" that would impress itself on others. This involved good works, sound doctrine, a seriousness of attitude, and sound speech that no one—not even the enemy—could condemn. Whether we like it or not, there are "contrary" people who are always looking for a fight.

A pastor's speech should be such that he stands without rebuke.

—*Be Faithful*, page 125

9. Paul challenges Titus to set "an example" (Titus 2:7). According to the rest of Titus, what would that example look like? How is this a picture of the "ideal" church leader?

From the Commentary

The believer should not have a bad attitude toward the government and show it by slanderous accusations and pugnacious actions. The word *gentle* (Titus 3:2) means "an attitude of moderation, a sweet reasonableness." Christians with this quality do not insist on the letter of the law, but are willing to compromise where no moral issue is at stake.

Again, Paul linked duty to doctrine. "Don't be too critical of your pagan neighbors," he wrote. "Just remember what you were before God saved you!" Titus 3:3 needs little explanation; we know what it means from our own experience.

—Be Faithful, page 129

10. What kinds of problems would prompt Paul to ask Titus to remind the people to be subject to "rulers and authorities"? Why is it so easy for believers to ignore that reminder? What is the difference between confidence in what you believe and disregard for the beliefs or authority of others?

More to Consider: Read Titus 3:9–11. What does this, the original "three strikes, you're out" rule, tell us about the persistence of disagreement in the church of Crete? Should churches today follow a similar guideline? How would they do that fairly and effectively and yet still show love to the guilty parties?

Looking Inward

Take a moment to reflect on all that you've explored thus far in this study of the book of Titus. Review your notes and answers and think about how each of these things matters in your life today.

Tips for Small Groups: To get the most out of this section, form pairs or trios and have group members take turns answering these questions. Be honest and as open as you can in this discussion, but most of all, be encouraging and supportive of others. Be sensitive to those who are going through particularly difficult times and don't press people to speak if they're uncomfortable doing so.

11. In what ways is your own spiritual life like that of the Christians in Crete? What false teachings tempt you away from the gospel of grace Paul preaches in his letters?

12. How do you determine what is "sound doctrine" in your own faith life? Do you examine the teachings of the church if something arises that you aren't familiar with? Why or why not? What steps can you take to test questionable teaching by leaders who influence your faith walk?

13. What are some of the passions that enslaved you in the past? What are some you're struggling with today? How can Paul's words to Titus in Titus 3:4–7 help you face these issues? What are some practical steps you can take to do what is good and right?

Going Forward

14. Think of one or two things you have learned that you'd like to work on in the coming week. Remember that this is all about quality, not quantity. It's better to work on one specific area of life and do it well than to work on many and do poorly (or to be so overwhelmed that you simply don't try).

Do you need to evaluate the teaching you're currently getting to make sure it's sound doctrine? Be specific. Go back through the book of Titus and put a star next to the phrase or verse that is most encouraging to you. Consider memorizing this verse.

Real-Life Application Ideas: Do a little research on church splits to determine what sorts of things caused the division. What common threads do you find? What mistakes were made by the leaders and members of those splitting churches? What can you learn from these stories to help you and your church maintain unity of purpose? Consider inviting conversation on these issues with your leadership as a preemptive measure to keep the church together and focused on its mission.

Seeking Help

15. Write a prayer below (or simply pray one in silence), inviting God to work on your mind and heart in those areas you've previously noted. Be honest about your desires and fears.

Notes for Small Groups:

- *Look for ways to put into practice the things you wrote in the Going Forward section. Talk with other group members about your ideas and commit to being accountable to one another.*

- *During the coming week, ask the Holy Spirit to continue to reveal truth to you from what you've read and studied.*

- *Before you start the next lesson, read 2 Timothy 1—2. For more in-depth lesson preparation, read chapters 9 and 10, "Christians Courageous!" and "Getting the Picture," in* Be Faithful.

Practical Courage

(2 TIMOTHY 1—2)

Before you begin ...
- *Pray for the Holy Spirit to reveal truth and wisdom as you go through this lesson.*
- *Read 2 Timothy 1—2. This lesson references chapters 9 and 10 in* Be Faithful. *It will be helpful for you to have your Bible and a copy of the commentary available as you work through this lesson.*

Getting Started

From the Commentary

When Paul wrote the letter we know as 2 Timothy, his situation had changed drastically. He was now a prisoner in Rome and was facing certain death (2 Tim. 4:6). For one reason or another, almost all of Paul's associates in the ministry were gone and only Luke was at the apostle's side to assist him (2 Tim. 4:11). It was a dark hour indeed.

But Paul's great concern was not for himself; it was for Timothy and the success of the gospel ministry.

—*Be Faithful,* page 137

1. Go through the letter and circle clues or outright statements that speak to Paul's circumstance during the writing of 2 Timothy. How (if at all) does the fact that Paul is in prison and facing death affect the tone of his second letter to Timothy?

2. Choose one verse or phrase from 2 Timothy 1—2 that stands out to you. This could be something you're intrigued by, something that makes you uncomfortable, something that puzzles you, something that resonates with you, or just something you want to examine further. Write that here.

Going Deeper

From the Commentary

> The ministry of the gospel is no place for a "timid soul"
> who lacks enthusiasm. In fact, courageous enthusiasm is
> essential for success in *any* kind of work. Paul compared
> this attitude to stirring up a fire into full flame (2 Tim. 1:6
> NIV). We must not conclude that Timothy was backslidden or lacked spiritual fire. Rather, Paul was encouraging
> his associate to keep the fire burning brightly so that it
> might generate spiritual power in his life.
>
> —*Be Faithful,* page 138

3. What are the encouragements Paul gives Timothy in 2 Timothy 1:1–7?
How would these words offer comfort to Timothy as he faces the ongoing
challenges in the Ephesian church? How are these encouragements
appropriate for the church today?

More to Consider: "Unashamed" is an ongoing theme of 2 Timothy. Go through the book and underline the different places this theme appears. How does this "unashamed" message speak to Paul's imprisonment? How might these words have helped to carry the greater message to Timothy?

From the Commentary

God has called us by His grace (2 Tim. 1:9). We are part of a great eternal plan that God determined "before the world began." God knows the end from the beginning. He has purposes for His people to accomplish for His glory. Suffering is a part of His plan. Jesus Christ suffered in the will of God here on earth, and all those who trust in Him will also suffer.

The emphasis in this verse is on *grace*. God saved us; we did not save ourselves (Eph. 2:8–9; Titus 3:5). He called us, not on the basis of our good works, but wholly on the basis of His grace. It is His purposes that we are to fulfill, and if these purposes include suffering, then we can accept it by faith and know that God's will is best. This is not fatalism. It is confidence in the wise plan of our gracious heavenly Father.

—Be Faithful, page 142

4. Why does Paul make a point to speak of God's grace in 2 Timothy 1:9? How does God's grace respond to suffering? How does this message speak also to the challenges Timothy was facing when Paul wrote 1 Timothy?

From the History Books

Paul isn't the only man noted for having written letters from prison. Famed theologian and Lutheran pastor Dietrich Bonhoeffer wrote many letters from prison while serving a sentence for opposing the German state. During the two years of his imprisonment (he was eventually hanged by the Nazi government), he wrote many letters that have been collected in the book *Letters and Papers from Prison*. Though the topics of his letters varied, he often wrote about what some have referred to as "religionless Christianity," a sometimes-controversial examination of what Christianity might look like "all grown up." Previously, Bonhoeffer had written the oft-quoted *The Cost of Discipleship*, an in-depth theological challenge to the idea of "cheap grace."

5. How do you think imprisonment might have influenced Bonhoeffer's thoughts on Christianity? In what ways was his imprisonment a validation of his earlier theological examination of "cheap grace"? How is this similar to Paul's circumstance? (See 2 Tim. 1:8.)

From the Commentary

The word *form* (2 Tim. 1:13) means "a pattern, an architect's sketch." There was a definite outline of doctrine in the early church, a standard by which teaching was tested. If Timothy changed this outline or abandoned it, then he would have nothing by which to test other teachers and preachers. We today need to hold fast to what Paul taught for the same reason.

However, note that Timothy's orthodoxy was to be tempered with "faith and love." "Speaking the truth in love" (Eph. 4:15) is the divine pattern. How easy it is to become pugnacious in our desire to defend the faith, or a witch-hunter who creates problems.

—*Be Faithful*, page 145

6. What is the "pattern of sound teaching" Paul encourages Timothy to pursue? What happens when leaders veer from that pattern? Name some examples of this in church history and in your own experience. How does one go about guarding the "good deposit" (2 Tim. 1:13–14)?

From the Commentary

> The ministry is not something we get for ourselves and keep to ourselves. We are stewards of the spiritual treasure God has given us. It is our responsibility to guard the deposit and then invest it in the lives of others. They, in turn, are to share the Word with the next generation of believers.
>
> It is important that we get our original treasure from the Word of God, and not from the ideas and philosophies of men. We do not test modern teachers by their popularity, education, or skill. We test them by the Word of God, and particularly the doctrines of grace as given by Paul. It is not we who examine Paul to see if he is right; it is Paul who examines us!
>
> *—Be Faithful,* page 151

7. Review 2 Timothy 2:1–7. Why do you think Paul uses three different illustrations in this passage (military, athletic, and farming)? How would each of these illustrations have reached a different audience? What lesson is there for today's church in this passage and in the way Paul presents it?

More to Consider: How does Paul's statement that no one wins unless he competes "according to the rules" line up with his overall theme of grace versus legalism (2 Tim. 2:5)? What does it look like to play according to the rules for teachers and leaders in the church?

From the Commentary

From the human point of view, Paul was a loser. There was nobody in the grandstands cheering him, for "all they which are in Asia" had turned away from him (2 Tim. 1:15). He was in prison, suffering as an evildoer. Yet *Paul was a winner!* He had kept the rules laid down in the Word of God, and one day he would get his reward from Jesus Christ. Paul was saying to young Timothy, "The important thing is that you obey the Word of God, no matter what the people may say. You are not running the race to please people or get fame. You are running to please Jesus Christ."

—*Be Faithful*, pages 154–55

8. Go through 2 Timothy and note the phrases Paul uses that naysayers might extract in order to mark Paul as a "loser." How did Paul take advantage of his challenging circumstances to exemplify and teach about God's grace?

*More to Consider: What is the "large house" Paul references in
2 Timothy 2:19–21? What makes the house stand firm? What
illustrations does he use to distinguish between the human aspect
of the Christian life and the godly aspect (see* Be Faithful, *pages
158–59, for insight)? Why is it important for the honorable
articles (or "vessels" in some translations) to be separated from the
dishonorable ones?*

From the Commentary

For God to be able to use us as vessels, we must be empty,
clean, and available. He will take us and fill us and use us
for His glory. But if we are filled with sin or defiled by dis-
obedience, He will first have to purge us, and that might
not be an enjoyable experience. In the "great house" of the
professing church, there are true believers and false. We
must exercise spiritual discernment and be careful that we
are vessels sanctified unto honor.

—*Be Faithful*, page 160

9. How does a Christian become an "empty vessel"? What steps do we
need to take for God to be able to use us most effectively? How does Paul
speak to the specifics of this in 2 Timothy 2:22–26?

From the Commentary

> A servant of God must instruct those who oppose him,
> for this is the only way he can rescue them from Satan's
> captivity. Satan is a liar (John 8:44). He captures people
> by his lying promises, as he did Eve (see Gen. 3; 2 Cor.
> 11:3). A servant's purpose is not to win arguments but to
> win souls. He wants to see deceived persons brought to
> repentance ("I was wrong—I have changed my mind")
> and the acknowledging of the truth.
>
> —*Be Faithful*, page 161

10. Paul refers to the "Lord's servant" in 2 Timothy 2:24. Why do you
think he uses the term "servant" in this context? What does it mean to be
the Lord's servant? What are the expectations of the Lord's servant when it
comes to correcting others?

Looking Inward

Take a moment to reflect on all that you've explored thus far in this study
of 2 Timothy 1—2. Review your notes and answers and think about how
each of these things matters in your life today.

Tips for Small Groups: To get the most out of this section, form pairs or trios and have group members take turns answering these questions. Be honest and as open as you can in this discussion, but most of all, be encouraging and supportive of others. Be sensitive to those who are going through particularly difficult times and don't press people to speak if they're uncomfortable doing so.

11. Paul says (in so many words) that the work of the gospel isn't for timid souls. In what ways have you been timid about your faith? Why is it sometimes difficult to speak boldly about what you believe? What might Paul say to you about the manner in which you live out and express your faith in Christ?

12. What are some of the ways you keep "the pattern of sound teaching" in your faith life? What practical steps do you take to make sure you're following sound doctrine? What, if any, questionable teachings are you wrestling with? How will you go about discovering the truth about these teachings?

13. How well are you following the teaching of 2 Timothy 2:22–26? What are the "evil desires of youth" that continue to tempt you? What are some practical ways you can pursue righteousness, faith, love, and peace?

Going Forward

14. Think of one or two things you have learned that you'd like to work on in the coming week. Remember that this is all about quality, not quantity. It's better to work on one specific area of life and do it well than to work on many and do poorly (or to be so overwhelmed that you simply don't try).

Do you need to work on developing courage in your faith? Study more about sound doctrine? Be specific. Go back through 2 Timothy 1—2 and put a star next to the phrase or verse that is most encouraging to you. Consider memorizing this verse.

Real-Life Application Ideas: Do something courageous that stretches your faith. You might consider joining an evangelistic team that reaches out to the homeless or going on a mission trip where you'll be called upon to share what you believe. During this experience, listen for God's voice as He gives you the strength and wisdom to boldly proclaim the gospel of grace.

Seeking Help

15. Write a prayer below (or simply pray one in silence), inviting God to work on your mind and heart in those areas you've previously noted. Be honest about your desires and fears.

Notes for Small Groups:

- *Look for ways to put into practice the things you wrote in the Going Forward section. Talk with other group members about your ideas and commit to being accountable to one another.*

- *During the coming week, ask the Holy Spirit to continue to reveal truth to you from what you've read and studied.*

- *Before you start the next lesson, read 2 Timothy 3—4. For more in-depth lesson preparation, read chapters 11 and 12, "What to Do Before It Ends" and "Last Words," in* Be Faithful.

Last Words
(2 TIMOTHY 3—4)

Before you begin …
- *Pray for the Holy Spirit to reveal truth and wisdom as you go through this lesson.*
- *Read 2 Timothy 3—4. This lesson references chapters 11 and 12 in* Be Faithful. *It will be helpful for you to have your Bible and a copy of the commentary available as you work through this lesson.*

Getting Started

From the Commentary

The emphasis in [2 Timothy 3] is on *knowledge* and *responsibility*. Paul informed Timothy about the character of the last days, and then instructed him how to respond. Action must be based on knowledge. Too many Christians are like the pilot who informed his passengers, "We are lost, but we are making very good time."

"These last days" began with the ministry of Jesus Christ (Heb. 1:1–2) and will continue until He returns. They are called the "last days" because in them God is completing His purposes for His people. Because our Lord has delayed His return, some people scoff at the promise of His coming (2 Peter 3:3ff.), but He will come as He promised.

—Be Faithful, page 165

1. In what ways does 2 Timothy speak to the issue of responsibility? Why would this be an important theme to share with Timothy, in light of Timothy's role as leader in the Ephesian church?

2. Choose one verse or phrase from 2 Timothy 3—4 that stands out to you. This could be something you're intrigued by, something that makes you uncomfortable, something that puzzles you, something that resonates with you, or just something you want to examine further. Write that here.

Going Deeper

From the Commentary

> A faithful believer should have nothing to do with the people Paul described in [2 Timothy 3:1–9]. It is important to note that these people operate *under the guise of religion:* "Having a form of godliness, but denying the power thereof" (2 Tim. 3:5). They are "religious" but rebellious!
>
> —*Be Faithful,* page 166

3. Go through 2 Timothy 3:1–9 and underline three facts about the "false" believers. This theme of false believers is a corollary to Paul's repeated challenges about "false teachers." How is it possible that people like this participate in the church? How is the warning Paul gives applicable to today's church?

From the Commentary

> "Lovers of pleasure more than lovers of God" does not
> suggest that we must choose between pleasure and God,
> for when we live for God, we enjoy the greatest pleasures
> (Ps. 16:11). The choice is between loving pleasure and
> loving God. If we love God, we will also enjoy fullness
> of life here and forever, but the pleasures of sin can only
> last for a brief time (Heb. 11:25). No one can deny that
> we live in a pleasure-mad world; but these pleasures too
> often are just shallow entertainment and escape; they are
> not enrichment and true enjoyment.
>
> —*Be Faithful*, page 168

4. Respond to Wiersbe's statement, "The choice is between loving pleasure
and loving God." Why do many nonbelievers think Christians are "no
fun"? How is this related to an improper reading of the message about
pleasure in 2 Timothy 3:4?

From Today's World

Many public figures who get lots of "face time" in news media do so because of their questionable financial practices. Those who claim no association with Christ still might be reviled by the general public for underhanded ways and greedy business dealings, but any who claim a relationship with Christ are typically given a harder time by the press. This is due in part, certainly, to the fact that most of these public figures claim nonprofit status and any evidence of personal wealth ought to put that status into question.

5. Why do you think those claiming to be believers are attacked more viciously by the press than those who don't claim a faith connection? What does this say about the media's beliefs about Christians? Are Christians held to a higher standard in other areas of life? Why or why not? In what ways is this a good thing? How can it make the message of grace more difficult to share with the world?

From the Commentary

Paul turned from the false leaders to remind Timothy that he (Paul) had been a faithful servant of God. It is

important in these difficult days that we follow the right
spiritual leaders.

—*Be Faithful*, page 170

6. Go through 2 Timothy 3:10–11 and underline the characteristics of
godly spiritual leaders as noted in Paul's description of his own way of life.
How do you see these characteristics in the leaders of the early church?
In the leaders of your local church? What persecutions and sufferings do
today's leaders endure for the sake of the gospel?

*More to Consider: Based on all you've read in Paul's letters, how
well do you think he'd stack up in comparison with other candidates
for the pastoral job in your church? What about Paul makes him a
great pastoral candidate? What are the things about his story and life
that might make the decision difficult for board members and church
members alike? What does this tell us about the very gospel of grace
that Paul preaches?*

From the Commentary

> Timothy had been taught the Word of God from the time
> he was a child. Some people are prone to say, "Well, I
> needed the Bible when I was younger, but I can do with-
> out it now that I'm older." How wrong they are! Adults
> need the guidance of the Word far more than children
> do, because adults face more temptations and make
> more decisions. Timothy's grandmother and mother had
> faithfully taught him the Old Testament Scriptures. (The
> word *whom* in 2 Tim. 3:14 is plural, referring to these
> women; see 2 Tim. 1:5.) Timothy was to continue in what
> he had been taught. We never outgrow the Word of God.
>
> —*Be Faithful*, page 172

7. Respond to the following statement: "We never outgrow the Word of
God." How does Paul underscore this truth in 2 Timothy 3:13–17?

From the Commentary

"Make full proof of thy ministry" [2 Tim. 4:5] means "fulfill whatever God wants you to do." Timothy's ministry would not be exactly like Paul's, but it would be important to the cause of Christ. No God-directed ministry is small or unimportant. In this final chapter, Paul named some colaborers about whom we know nothing; yet they too had a ministry to fulfill.

A young preacher once complained to Charles Spurgeon, the famous British preacher of the 1800s, that he did not have as big a church as he deserved.

"How many do you preach to?" Spurgeon asked.

"Oh, about a hundred," the man replied.

Solemnly Spurgeon said, "That will be enough to give account for on the day of judgment."

—*Be Faithful*, page 182

8. What is the "work of an evangelist" Paul refers to in 2 Timothy 4:5? What sorts of hardships did Paul and the early church pastors endure that today's pastors rarely face? What are the unique challenges of today's generation of pastors?

More to Consider: Paul references a number of specific people in the closing of his second letter to Timothy. What does this say about Paul's ministry? About Timothy's work? What implications does it have for pastors today?

From the Commentary

> When Paul had been discouraged in Corinth, the Lord came to him and encouraged him (Acts 18:9–11). After he had been arrested in Jerusalem, Paul again was visited by the Lord and encouraged (Acts 23:11). During that terrible storm, when Paul was on board a ship, the Lord had again given him strength and courage (Acts 27:22ff.). Now, in that horrible Roman prison, Paul again experienced the strengthening presence of the Lord, who had promised, "I will never leave thee, nor forsake thee" (Heb. 13:5).
>
> —*Be Faithful*, page 186

9. Where does Paul's confidence in God's nearness come from? (Read Acts 18:9–11; 23:11; 27:21–26. What was unique about each of these experiences?) Is it foolishness or faithfulness that allows Paul to trust that God will once again be there for him? How is Paul's comment that the Lord will bring him "safely to his heavenly kingdom" particularly telling about Paul's dire situation in prison? How can Paul's confidence help build our own confidence in God's nearness?

From the Commentary

> It is heartening to see how many people are named in the
> closing part of this last letter Paul wrote. I believe that
> there are at least one hundred different men and women
> named in Acts and Paul's letters, as part of his circle of
> friends and fellow laborers. Paul could not do the job by
> himself. It is a great man who enlists others to help get
> the job done, and who lets them share in the greatness of
> the work.
>
> —*Be Faithful*, page 187

10. Go through 2 Timothy 4:9–22 and circle the names of all the people
Paul mentions. What clues do we get from Paul's words about the character
of these pastors and fellow laborers? If Paul were to write a similar closing
to your church, what sort of list might he include? Who are the people in
your community who qualify as fellow laborers?

Looking Inward

Take a moment to reflect on all that you've explored thus far in this study of 2 Timothy 3—4. Review your notes and answers and think about how each of these things matters in your life today.

Tips for Small Groups: To get the most out of this section, form pairs or trios and have group members take turns answering these questions. Be honest and as open as you can in this discussion, but most of all, be encouraging and supportive of others. Be sensitive to those who are going through particularly difficult times and don't press people to speak if they're uncomfortable doing so.

11. What are some specific things you've observed or experienced that suggest we are in the "last days" Paul talks about in 2 Timothy 3:1–9? What does the "last days" mean to you? How does considering the "last days" affect the way you live your life in the now?

12. What persecutions have you faced because of your faith? If you haven't experienced any, why is that? If you have, how did you respond to those persecutions? What can you learn from the manner in which Paul

responded to persecution that will prepare you for any future challenges to your faith?

13. Paul challenges Timothy to preach the word and "be prepared in season and out of season" for Christ's return. In what ways is Paul's charge to Timothy applicable to your own life? What does it look like, practically speaking, to be prepared for Christ's return? How can you "keep your head in all situations"?

Going Forward

14. Think of one or two things you have learned that you'd like to work on in the coming week. Remember that this is all about quality, not quantity. It's better to work on one specific area of life and do it well than to work on many and do poorly (or to be so overwhelmed that you simply don't try).

Do you need to spend more time in Scripture so you can be wise in the face of challenges to your faith? Be specific. Go back through 2 Timothy 3—4 and put a star next to the phrase or verse that is most encouraging to you. Consider memorizing this verse.

Real-Life Application Ideas: Take a few minutes to imagine how you might change the way you're living if you knew Christ was returning in the next month or year. Would you change the way you relate to family members? Coworkers? Strangers? How does a sense of urgency or "advent" impact the way in which you live out your faith?

Seeking Help

15. Write a prayer below (or simply pray one in silence), inviting God to work on your mind and heart in those areas you've previously noted. Be honest about your desires and fears.

Notes for Small Groups:

- *Look for ways to put into practice the things you wrote in the Going Forward section. Talk with other group members about your ideas and commit to being accountable to one another.*

- *During the coming week, ask the Holy Spirit to continue to reveal truth to you from what you've read and studied.*

- *Before you start the next lesson, read the book of Philemon. For more in-depth lesson preparation, read chapter 13, "A Tale of Two Cities," in* Be Faithful.

Two Cities
(PHILEMON)

Before you begin ...
- *Pray for the Holy Spirit to reveal truth and wisdom as you go through this lesson.*
- *Read Philemon. This lesson references chapter 13 in* Be Faithful. *It will be helpful for you to have your Bible and a copy of the commentary available as you work through this lesson.*

Getting Started

From the Commentary

Paul was a prisoner in Rome, his friend Philemon was in Colossae, and the human link between them was a runaway slave named Onesimus. The details are not clear, but it appears that Onesimus robbed his master and then fled to Rome, hoping to be swallowed up in the crowded metropolis. But, in the providence of God, he met Paul and was converted!

—*Be Faithful,* page 195

1. What are your impressions of Paul based solely on his greeting and prayer in verses 1–7? How does the manner in which he opens this letter help to set the table for what he is about to say to Philemon about his runaway slave?

2. Choose one verse or phrase from Philemon that stands out to you. This could be something you're intrigued by, something that makes you uncomfortable, something that puzzles you, something that resonates with you, or just something you want to examine further. Write that here.

Going Deeper

From the Commentary

> Along with the epistle to the Colossians, this letter prob-
> ably was carried to Colossae by Tychicus and Onesimus
> (Col. 4:7–9). In it, we see Paul in three important roles as
> he tried to help Philemon solve his problems. At the same
> time, we see a beautiful picture of what the Father has
> done for us in Jesus Christ. Martin Luther said, "All of us
> are Onesimuses!" and he was right.
>
> —*Be Faithful*, page 195

3. What are the different roles Paul plays in order to help Philemon with
his problem? In what ways are we all "Onesimuses," as Martin Luther once
said?

From the Commentary

> In his greeting, Paul expressed his deep love for his
> Christian friends, and he reminded them that he was a
> prisoner for Jesus Christ (see also Philem. 9–10, 13, 23).

Timothy was included in the greeting, though the burden of the letter was from the heart of Paul to the heart of Philemon. Paul's ministry was a "team" operation, and he often included the names of his associates when he wrote his letters.

—*Be Faithful*, page 196

4. Read the following Scripture passages: Romans 16:3, 9, 21; 1 Corinthians 3:9; Philippians 2:25; 4:3; Colossians 4:11. What do you learn from Paul's repeated use of the term "fellow worker"? What do you think Paul means when he calls Philemon his "fellow worker" in Philemon 1?

From the History Books

Though its origins are ancient, Americans know about slavery primarily because it divided a nation and led to the Civil War, which ultimately resulted in slavery's abolishment. In the time of Paul, slavery was rarely if ever questioned—it was simply part of the culture. But one thing that didn't change much between the first century and the nineteenth is the value that slave owners put on their slaves. Before the end of slavery in America, it wasn't uncommon for slave owners to offer significant rewards for the capture of runaway slaves—as high as $1,000 (which was an enormous amount of money at the time). The reason for the large rewards was simple: A slave offered essentially a lifetime of free labor (and promised future generations of free labor as well). To lose a slave was to lose the equivalent of a large sum of money. Of course, slaves who were captured were usually punished (often severely) in order to teach them a lesson.

5. What do you know about other similarities and differences between slavery in the first century and in the nineteenth? How might the slave owners in nineteenth-century America have responded to Paul's plea in this letter?

More to Consider: The New Testament churches met in homes (see Rom. 16:5, 23; 1 Cor. 16:19), so it's possible Philemon's home was also a place of worship. Philemon certainly would have known about Paul's influence and ministry, even though Paul likely never made it to the Colossian church. How might receiving a letter from Paul have made an impression on Philemon?

From the Commentary

> If a slave ran away, the master would register the name
> and description with the officials, and the slave would be
> on the "wanted" list. Any free citizen who found a run-
> away slave could assume custody and even intercede with
> the owner. The slave was not automatically returned to
> the owner, nor was he automatically sentenced to death.
> While it is true that some masters were cruel (one man
> threw his slave into a pool of man-eating fish!), many of
> them were reasonable and humane.
>
> —*Be Faithful*, page 197

6. What must it have been like for Onesimus to be on a "wanted" list?
What made it possible for him to even consider returning to his owner?
What do you think Paul said to Onesimus after his conversion that led to
the writing of this letter?

From the Commentary

> The word translated "partner" is *koinonia*, which means "to have in common." It is translated "communication" in Philemon 6, which means "fellowship." Paul volunteered to become a "business partner" with Philemon and help him solve the problem with Onesimus. He made two suggestions: "Receive him as myself," and "Put that [whatever he stole from you] on my account."
>
> —*Be Faithful*, page 199

7. How are Paul's suggestions for dealing with Onesimus in Philemon 17–21 illustrative of what Jesus has done for us as believers?

From the Commentary

> Paul did not suggest that Philemon ignore the slave's crimes and forget about the debt Onesimus owed. Rather, Paul offered to pay the debt himself. "Put it on my account—I will repay it!" The language in Philemon 19

sounds like a legal promissory note of that time. This was Paul's assurance to his friend that the debt would be paid.

It takes more than love to solve the problem; love must pay a price.

—*Be Faithful*, page 200

8. What sort of debts did Paul offer to pay on behalf of Onesimus? What was the price Jesus paid for *our* crimes?

From the Commentary

Philemon 19 suggests that it was Paul who led Philemon to faith in Christ. Paul used this special relationship to encourage his friend to receive Onesimus. Philemon and Onesimus were not only spiritual brothers in the Lord, but they had the same "spiritual father"—Paul! (See Philem. 10 and 1 Cor. 4:15.)

—*Be Faithful*, page 200

9. What does Paul's relationship with Onesimus tell us about the role of trust in relationships? How was their shared faith a factor in the decision that led to the writing of this letter and the offer of Onesimus's safe, unpunished return to his master? Consider Paul's reasoning in Philemon 15–16. Why does Paul offer this possible explanation to Philemon?

From the Commentary

Had the early Christians begun an open crusade against slavery, they would have been crushed by the opposition, and the message of the gospel would have become confused with a social and political program. Think of how difficult it was for people to overcome slavery in England and America, and those two nations had general education and the Christian religion to help prepare the way. Think also of the struggles in the modern Civil Rights movement even within the church.

—*Be Faithful*, pages 201–2

10. What, if anything, about this book of the Bible troubles you? Why didn't Paul champion a cause against slavery? Why is it important to

consider the context of the culture when studying Scripture? How is the letter to Philemon a good example of this?

Looking Inward

Take a moment to reflect on all that you've explored thus far in this study of the book of Philemon. Review your notes and answers and think about how each of these things matters in your life today.

Tips for Small Groups: To get the most out of this section, form pairs or trios and have group members take turns answering these questions. Be honest and as open as you can in this discussion, but most of all, be encouraging and supportive of others. Be sensitive to those who are going through particularly difficult times and don't press people to speak if they're uncomfortable doing so.

11. In what ways are you participating on a "team" of ministers, as it is clear Paul was from his greeting? Why is that important? If you are a "lone ranger" in ministry, what can you do to change that? What are some ways you can partner with others to share the gospel of grace?

12. Think of a time you were forgiven for a wrong. What did it feel like to be forgiven when you ought to have been punished? How is that like Onesimus's story? How is that a type or shadow of the forgiveness Jesus offers?

13. Paul asks Philemon to welcome Onesimus back as if welcoming Paul himself. When have you experienced this sort of unexpected or undeserved welcome? How is this like being welcomed into the family of God?

Going Forward

14. Think of one or two things you have learned that you'd like to work on in the coming week. Remember that this is all about quality, not quantity. It's better to work on one specific area of life and do it well than to work on many and do poorly (or to be so overwhelmed that you simply don't try).

Do you need to work on being more forgiving? Do you need to learn how to better accept God's grace? Be specific. Go back through the book of Philemon and put a star next to the phrase or verse that is most encouraging to you. Consider memorizing this verse.

Real-Life Application Ideas: If someone has wronged you or taken something from you, think about what it would look like to offer complete forgiveness to that person (if you haven't already). It may or may not be necessary to contact that person and tell him or her about your offer of forgiveness (forgiveness is something that mostly happens in the heart of the forgiver). Share your story with a trusted friend and then spend time praying together for you to truly be able to forgive without any lingering grudge.

Seeking Help

15. Write a prayer below (or simply pray one in silence), inviting God to work on your mind and heart in those areas you've previously noted. Be honest about your desires and fears.

Notes for Small Groups:

- *Look for ways to put into practice the things you wrote in the Going Forward section. Talk with other group members about your ideas and commit to being accountable to one another.*
- *During the coming week, ask the Holy Spirit to continue to reveal truth to you from what you've read and studied.*

Summary and Review

Notes for Small Groups: This session is a summary and review of this book. Because of that, it is shorter than the previous lessons. If you are using this in a small-group setting, consider combining this lesson with a time of fellowship or a shared meal.

Before you begin ...
- *Pray for the Holy Spirit to reveal truth and wisdom as you go through this lesson.*
- *Briefly review the notes you made in the previous sessions. You will refer back to previous sections throughout this bonus lesson.*

Looking Back

1. Over the past eight lessons, you've examined four of Paul's letters. What expectations did you bring to this study? In what ways were these expectations met?

2. What is the most significant personal discovery you made from this study?

3. What surprised you most about Paul's letters? Which of the letters spoke most directly to a need in your own life? How?

Progress Report

4. Take a few moments to review the Going Forward sections of the previous lessons. How would you rate your progress for each of the things you chose to work on? What adjustments, if any, do you need to make to continue on the path toward spiritual maturity?

5. In what ways have you grown closer to Christ during this study? Take a moment to celebrate those things. Then think of areas where you feel you still need to grow and note those here. Make plans to revisit this study in a few weeks to review your growing faith.

Things to Pray About

6. All four of Paul's letters were written to deal with specific issues in the early church—from false teachers to the acceptance of a runaway slave. As you reflect on the words Paul has written, ask God to reveal to you those truths that you most need to hear. Revisit the book often and seek the Holy Spirit's guidance to gain a better understanding of what it means to be righteous before God.

7. Make a quick list of the main themes in 1 and 2 Timothy, Titus, and Philemon. Then consider how each of these themes is applicable to your life today. Spend time praying for each of these topics.

8. Whether you've been studying this in a small group or on your own, there are many other Christians working through the very same issues you discovered when examining Paul's letters. Take time to pray for each of them, that God would reveal truth, that the Holy Spirit would guide you, and that each person might grow in spiritual maturity according to God's will.

A Blessing of Encouragement

Studying the Bible is one of the best ways to learn how to be more like Christ. Thanks for taking this step. In closing, let this blessing precede

you and follow you into the next week while you continue to marinate in God's Word:

May God light your path to greater understanding as you review the truths found in 1 and 2 Timothy, Titus, and Philemon and consider how they can help you grow closer to Christ.